The Book of Ruth
A study in Redemption and Christian Living

Katherine Ford

Scripture Truth Publications

FIRST EDITION

FIRST PRINTING July 2024

ISBN: 978-0-901860-03-3 (paperback)

Copyright © 2023 Katherine Ford and Scripture Truth Publications

An STP publication

All rights reserved. No part of this publication may be reproduced, stored in a retrieval system, or transmitted, in any form or by any means, electronic, mechanical, photocopying, recording or otherwise without prior permission of Scripture Truth Publications.

Katherine Ford has asserted his right under the Copyright, Designs and Patents Act 1988 to be identified as author of this work.

Scripture quotations, unless otherwise indicated, are taken from the New King James Version®(NKJV). Copyright © 1982 by Thomas Nelson. Used by permission. All rights reserved.

Scripture quotations marked (NIV) are taken from The Holy Bible, New International Version Anglicised. Copyright © 1979, 1984, 2011 Biblica. Used by permission of Hodder & Stoughton Ltd, an Hachette UK company. All rights reserved. 'NIV' is a registered trademark of Biblica. UK trademark number 1448790

Scripture quotations marked (ESV) are from the ESV® Bible (The Holy Bible, English Standard Version®, copyright © 2001 by Crossway, a publishing ministry of Good News Publishers. Used by permission. All rights reserved.

Scripture quotations marked (NLT) are taken from the *Holy Bible*, New Living Translation, copyright ©1996, 2004, 2015 by Tyndale House Foundation. Used by permission of Tyndale House Publishers, Carol Stream, Illinois 60188. All rights reserved.

Scripture quotations marked (ICB) are taken from the International Children's Bible®. Copyright © 1986, 1988, 1999 by Thomas Nelson. Used by permission. All rights reserved.

Scripture quotations marked (Darby) are taken from The Holy Scriptures, Darby Translation, accessed through biblegateway.com

Scripture quotations marked (ASV) are taken from The Holy Bible, American Standard Version accessed through biblegateway.com

Dedication

To my brothers – without access to whose libraries either this book or my bank account would be much the poorer.

Contents

Preface	7
Introduction	10
Chapter 1	17
Chapter 2	28
Chapter 3	38
Chapter 4	47
How does the Book of Ruth point to Jesus?	57
Bibiliography and tools used	65
About the author	67

Preface

Recently, I've been discovering how lazy a Bible student I've been. Yes, I had read the Bible, attended Bible teaching meetings, read plenty of books (I enjoy reading) and listened to teaching online. All of these activities are good in and of themselves, but do they count as studying? Well maybe yes and no. I'm not intending to give the impression that doing these things is bad or that we shouldn't do them – we should. But for me, too often there was a gap between hearing or reading and actually studying. I'd read or listened and (sometimes) was able to answer questions immediately afterwards about the content, but then what was learnt would soon be forgotten. Too often what was being read or heard wasn't being broken down, analysed and put back together to form a functional knowledge base. I've been a lazy student, only too willing to be spoon-fed and follow other people's opinions and theories, rather than studying for myself, thinking about things and making my own judgements.

For those who aren't like me and are wondering what on earth I'm talking about, that's great! Keep doing, learning, studying and growing in the way that works for you – as long as it actually works and results in growth. For those who may be a bit like me, let's find ways of becoming better Bible students. Let's become like the Bereans (see Acts 17:11); we should be eager to learn from the Scriptures, making the most of teachers, commentators and peers, but then examining what we hear or read for ourselves to ensure what we are learning is in accordance with God's Word.

What I've found helpful in this area are study guides that give homework. Yes, we groan at the idea of homework (and at the thought of it transporting us back to school days) but I've found that it actually helps me to think and study for myself about a topic before receiving the teaching from another. For me, this helps the lessons to sink in deeper – because I've actually had to put in some effort to find them – but also has the added benefit of encouragement when the answers I've come up with are in line with those then taught by the teacher.

As such, this study guide is set up in a similar way.

1. Each chapter starts by asking you to read through the whole book and then the appropriate chapter. For those short of time, you may wish just to read the appropriate chapter, but I really would encourage you to read the whole book each time (Ruth is only short). Repetitive reading not only helps us to put the chapter into context but also helps to highlight different aspects with each reading and sinks the lessons in deeper. (It can also help unconsciously with Scripture memory.) I'd also encourage you, if possible, to read Ruth in different translations of the Bible.

2. Next, there are a few questions about what will be studied in that chapter. The questions aren't there to trick or catch you out but to get you to think about the subject. There may not be right or wrong answers – what I draw out of a text may be different from what you find, and that's all right as long as they're in line with the whole of Scripture.

3. The chapter then presents what I've drawn out of the chapter with some suggested applications and learning points (all equally, if not more, relevant for me to learn and apply than for you).

4. Each chapter will then close with a few "Points for further thought and action". These are suggested lessons from the chapter that you may wish to think further about and find ways to apply to your life with a view to the learning becoming relevant and real. You may wish to add your own points to this section.

This book is designed to be usable for personal Bible study or for group study. Learning together has the added bonus of being able to discuss our findings with others and learn from what each other has found. It also helps with accountability – I'm far more likely actually to do the "homework" properly and in depth if I know I'm expected to provide feedback on it. In group settings, the idea would be for all to do the "homework" section individually and then gather together to discuss their findings, the content of the teaching part of the chapter and the "Points for further thought and action". For those for whom group study is not possible, don't worry. This book is still for you. I'd suggest writing down answers for the "homework" section (either in this book or on a separate note-pad) – again, because if you're anything like me, writing answers provides more accountability and motivation to do this part properly, which will help you get more out of it.

I hope that you enjoy this study as much as I've enjoyed doing the studying to prepare it. May we all become diligent students of God's Word, learning and applying the lessons that He has to teach us through the Book of Ruth.

The Book of Ruth – Introduction

Read through the whole Book of Ruth; then work through the questions below before reading the chapter.

❖ What does the book tell us about its author, and when and why it was written?

❖ The book is set in the time of the Judges (1:1). What do we know from the Book of Judges about these times (see Judges 2:10-23 for a summary)?

❖ What is the structure of the book? How would you split it up and what is each section about?

❖ What themes can you see in Ruth that are themes found in the rest of the Bible?

Introductions to studies of Bible books often begin with the Who, When, What, and Why questions of the book's authorship. The Book of Ruth, however, doesn't give away many clues to the answers to those questions. The identity of the author is not revealed. Unlike Luke's narratives (Luke 1:1-4; Acts 1:1), no purpose for telling this story is stated. As regards when it was written, it can be assumed that it was long enough after the events described to allow customs to change (Ruth 4:7) and that it was after David became king, since he is mentioned in the genealogies that conclude the book (4:17, 22), but that doesn't narrow it down greatly. Some suggest that it was written by Samuel, potentially with the ending added on at a later time, although there is no firm consensus on this. The author does provide some clues as to when the events occurred – "in the days when the judges ruled" 1:1 – though when in this period it was or which judge was ruling at the time is not stated.

In view of this, I'd like to suggest that, while a rough dating point helps us to understand some of what happens in the book and where it fits into the big picture of redemption history, the specifics of when, why and by whom the book was written are not key to our understanding. The focus should be on the God who is clearly orchestrating the events, rather than on the human narrator.

The times of the Judges

The period between the conquest of the Promised Land by the children of Israel and when Saul became King provides the backdrop for the scenes in the Book of Ruth. During this time, various judges were raised up to rule over the people, nationally or locally, as presented in the Book of Judges. Initially, Israel was united under Joshua and was committed to following God (Joshua 24:24). The Israelites began to conquer and take possession of the land and drive out their enemies, but never fully accomplished this.

Judges 2:6-23 provides a summary of this period. The people followed the Lord while Joshua and those of his generation were alive and could remember all that God had done for them. The next generation, however, had not personally witnessed God's deliverance and did not know Him. They went after the gods of the nations and turned away from God. He punished Israel for their disobedience and idolatry by allowing their enemies to attack and rule over them. This is where the judges came in. God would raise up a judge to save Israel from their enemies and bring about a period of rest. When the judge died, the cycle of rebellion, oppression, salvation and rest would begin again.

Many of the judges are presented as having various flaws or what were perceived as weaknesses at the time – Ehud was left-handed; Deborah, a woman; Gideon, full of doubts; Jephthah, an illegitimate outcast, etc. They were men and women whom God chose in spite of – or perhaps because of – their weaknesses to rule over His people and provide a way of salvation from their oppressors. Isn't it wonderful that God chooses to use flawed human beings as part of His master plan? As the Book of Judges progresses, there is a downward trend in the character of the nation and of its judges. We see Othniel in Judges 1 claiming possession of the land that God had promised and asking for more of an inheritance. In contrast, by the time we get to Samson in Judges 13-16, we see a total disregard for his Nazarite vows and little difference between him and the Philistines around him. And that's before we get to the tribe of Levi in the final chapters of the book, with those who were supposed to aid the people in the worship of God completely turning away from Him, and the consequent disintegration of society.

Twice in the final chapters of Judges (17:6; 21:25) comes the refrain summarising these times: "In those days there was no king in Israel; everyone did what was right in his own eyes". After the conquest of the land, Joshua presented the Israelites with a choice: would they serve God or would they choose to follow other gods (Joshua 24:15)? When the people claimed that they would serve the LORD, Joshua warned them of the enormity of what they were promising to do and of the consequences of breaking God's covenant, and yet Israel categorically committed to serving and obeying God (vv. 19-25). Fast-forward through the period of the judges and we get a complete U-turn! No longer is there a national commitment to Jehovah and following the Law; instead there is a culture of self-serving in which everyone is at liberty to define right and wrong. Before we judge the Israelites too harshly, how often are we like this today? Those New Year's Resolutions – how often we commit to something only to find that good intentions soon peter out in the business of daily living. When it comes to spiritual things and our commitment to following Jesus, do we continually sacrifice our lives to do His will (Romans 12:1) or do we waver and fall when the going gets tough?

Against this backdrop, the characters of Ruth and Boaz stand in stark contrast as we shall see later. While in our Bibles Ruth is found in its historical place immediately after the Book of Judges and before 1 Samuel, in some older collections Ruth was placed after Proverbs. It could be that the intention was for Ruth to stand as an illustration of the "wife of noble character" or "virtuous woman" as described in Proverbs 31.

The structure of the book

Ruth is split into four short chapters (the whole book is only 85 verses in total). In chapter 1, we see an Israelite family moving to Moab when there is famine in Israel. While they are there, death wipes out all but Naomi. She decides to return to Bethlehem and encourages her Moabite daughters-in-law to remain in Moab. Ruth, however, commits to staying with Naomi and to following God. Chapter 2 shows Ruth hard at work providing for herself and Naomi by gleaning during the harvest-time. She "just happens" to work in the fields belonging to Boaz, who in turn generously provides for and blesses the widows. By chapter 3 Naomi is planning how she can get security for Ruth and orchestrates a night-time proposal between Ruth and Boaz, counting on Boaz to redeem them by buying the family land, marrying Ruth and providing an heir. The final chapter sees Boaz legally settling the matter, marrying Ruth and experiencing the birth of their son.

The structure holds much symmetry:

- In the opening chapter, there is death and grief followed by a demonstration of loyalty and commitment. The final chapter begins with a demonstration of loyalty and commitment followed by new life and rejoicing.
- Chapters 2 and 3 both begin and end with discussions between Naomi and Ruth in their home, with a meeting between Ruth and Boaz in the middle.
- Chapter 2 shows how Ruth and Naomi resolved their immediate need for food. Chapter 3 shows how they resolved their longer-term need for security and a future.

Throughout the whole book, while the characters are often mentioning the LORD, the narrator makes only a couple of direct references to what God was doing (1:6; 4:13). There is, however, a constant undercurrent of how God is moving behind the scenes, both in the laws upon which much of the action is founded and in all the 'coincidences' in the story. Isn't this how it is in our lives today? We may not see God's hand at work in our lives at the time, as we're making decisions and using our free will. And yet there are times when we look back and hindsight shows how clearly God was at work, bringing things together at just the right time and closing other doors to achieve His purposes, and for His glory. In my mind, this is how life often is for the majority of us – God working concurrently with, apparently, our own decisions. We're not all like Moses, with God telling us through burning bushes what He wants us to do. We don't all have pillars of cloud and fire guiding us through the wildernesses of life, or angels telling us good news for our futures. Ruth provides the assurance that God is at work in ordinary, everyday life, and of the interplay between divine will and human responsibility.

Ruth also mirrors a common structure observed in the Bible. When providing an overview of redemption history, often the four points of Creation, Fall, Redemption and Restoration (or some equivalent) are used. The story begins by setting the scene, introducing Naomi and her family. Then some sort of crisis occurs – famine, death of family members and Naomi's and Ruth's perceived emptiness and hopelessness. A resolution is found to the crisis as Boaz becomes their kinsman-redeemer —a close relative who was willing and able to help them in their time of need (discussed in more detail later on). Finally, what was lost is restored and further blessings received, seen in the birth of Obed, and rejoicing as Naomi exchanges emptiness for fullness. This pattern can be seen in the lives of Joseph, Job and others. Ultimately, it points us to Jesus and the great story of our salvation (Philippians 2:5-11). This will be discussed further in a later chapter.

Themes in the Book of Ruth

Many of the themes that run through the tapestry of the Bible from the Creation to its close are present in the Book of Ruth.

1. Offspring – much of the book revolves around the crisis created by Naomi's and Ruth's lack of an heir to maintain the family name and inherit the land.

2. Land – God had allotted set portions of the land to each tribe and family when Israel conquered Canaan. There was great emphasis on keeping the land in the family and claiming possession. This was a problem when Naomi had no heir to claim Elimelech's land.

3. Rest – God rested following the Creation and instituted the Sabbath. The story of Ruth also revolves around finding

security and rest for Ruth and the one who would be able to provide it.

4. Redemption – Naomi and Ruth were in need of a redeemer. Boaz was to be their kinsman-redeemer.

These themes will be looked at in more detail in future chapters.

Points for further thought or action

❖ Looking back, can you see times when God has been at work behind the scenes in your life?

❖ The Israelites promised to follow the Lord and His Law, yet the times of the Judges show this promise wasn't kept. Does your life display your commitment to follow the Lord? If not, what needs changing to let this be the case?

Chapter 1

Read the Book of Ruth and then reread chapter 1.

❖ What do we know about Moab from earlier in the Bible (see Genesis 19:30-38 and Numbers 25)?

❖ Why does Naomi tell Ruth and Orpah to return to Moab and to their gods? What might this (and the rest of the chapter) tell us about Naomi's relationship with God at this point?

❖ What commitment does Ruth make?

❖ What does this chapter teach us about God (think beyond just the words used)? What names are used for God?

❖ Why does verse 22 tell us that it was the start of the barley harvest? What significance does this have?

Chapter 1 opens with a problem. Not only is the setting the time of the Judges (see Introduction) but there is a famine in the land. This land that was supposed to be flowing with "milk and honey" (Exodus 3:8) was experiencing famine. Ironic? Couple that with the town our characters are from - Bethlehem, which means "House of Bread". And yet this is the repeated lesson that history teaches. We're living in a world that God declared to be "good" and "very good", that has since been spoilt and broken by man's disobedience and rebellion against God (Genesis 1, 2). Eden, the garden of ease and plenty, received a curse that resulted in toil and futility. Similarly, the Promised Land of abundance became a land of famine following Israel's rebellion and turning away from God, a judgement Israel was warned about prior to entering the land (Deuteronomy 32:24).

Because of the famine, Elimelech and his family – wife Naomi and sons Mahlon and Chilion – move to Moab. Abraham and later Isaac similarly relocated during times of famine (Genesis 12, 26), yet neither relocation turned out particularly well for those involved. So it was with Elimelech. The Bible doesn't pass comment on whether Elimelech was right or wrong to move to Moab. It is generally seen, though, as a negative move rather than being positive or even neutral. To understand more of what this meant to those in Elimelech's day we need to look back at the Covenant God made with Abraham. In Genesis 13:15 and 17:8 God promised to give Abraham and his descendants the land of Canaan as "an everlasting possession" and that He would be their God. He also told Abraham that his descendants would first be enslaved in another land before returning to Canaan to claim their inheritance (Genesis 15:13-16). During the times of the Exodus and the wilderness wandering, there is a repeated focus on "the land which the LORD ... God is giving [them]" (e.g. Exodus 20:12) and statutes to implement once they inherit the land (e.g. Exodus 13:11-12; Leviticus 14:34ff; 19:23; Numbers 15:2-5). This emphasis on the land as part of the Covenant highlights the severity of Moses's generation being banned from entering it because of their refusal to trust God (Numbers 14:30).

On entering the land, each tribe was allotted their own portion to inherit and there was a strong focus on maintaining the land within the tribe. Rules were made, for example, to ensure land was not permanently sold (Leviticus 25:28) and that marriage didn't transfer inheritance out of the tribe (Numbers 36:7-9). The stories of Zelophehad's daughters (Numbers 27, 36; Joshua 17) and of Naboth's vineyard (1 Kings 21) underline this point. In this context, Elimelech's decision to leave his inheritance in the land of Israel became an even bigger decision than moving country would be for us today. Not only was he saying "goodbye" to family, friends and all he had known, he was also leaving behind the land allotted to him and his family by God.

Was Elimelech showing a lack of faith in God to meet his needs and those of his family during the famine? Did he feel that God wouldn't provide for them just because the land God had provided was fruitless? The Bible doesn't say and sometimes it's best for us not to speculate about motives and reasoning, judging those for whom no judgement is recorded. That said, given Israel's history with Moab, relocating there was an interesting decision. Elimelech could have moved the family to another part of Israel. He could have settled in the land on the east bank of the Jordan belonging to Israel rather than going to Moab. Why Moab?

Genesis tells us about the origins of the Moabites. After Abraham and Lot separated, Lot went to dwell in Sodom (Genesis 13:12). Later, because of the wickedness of the people in Sodom and its neighbour, Gomorrah, the Lord destroyed the cities (Genesis 19:13; 18:20-21; 19:23-25). Before the destruction came, however, God sent messengers to Sodom to take Lot and his family out of the city so that they could be spared (Genesis 19). Lot and his two daughters left Sodom and escape to Zoar. Lot's wife also left Sodom but disobeyed the LORD's messengers by turning to look back and was consequently turned into a pillar of salt (v. 26). Thus we see Lot and his two daughters isolated and displaced, afraid to stay in the city of Zoar – or presumably any other city – for fear of further retribution. The importance of family lines and inheritance then emerges as Lot's daughters scheme and plot how to ensure their family line is not cut off. Both daughters sleep with and become pregnant by Lot. The son of the elder daughter was called Moab and became the father of the Moabites (Genesis 19:37).

Fast-forward to the time of the Exodus and the Israelites are camped in the land of Moab on the eastern bank of the River Jordan, waiting to enter the Promised Land (Numbers 22:1). The Moabites are understandably nervous of the vast company lodging in their land and the potential for hostile repercussions (Israel having just defeated the neighbouring Amorites in Numbers 21). The Moabites need not have been afraid – God had instructed Moses not to attack or war with Moab since He had given the land to Moab and would not give Moab's portion to Israel (Deuteronomy 2:9). The king of Moab, Balak, decided to hire Balaam, a seer, to curse the Israelites so that the Moabites could then evict them from Moab (Numbers 22:6). After futile attempts to curse Israel, in which God causes Balaam to bless them instead, Balaam advises Balak that mingling with the Israelites may be the best plan to draw them away from God and ultimately defeat them (Numbers 31:16). Numbers 25 tells of how this advice was followed. The people of the two nations dwelt together and the Israelites were drawn into idolatry and immorality.

In Judges 3, we again see the hostility of Moab to Israel with the Moabite King Eglon subduing the Israelites for eighteen years before a deliverer was raised up to overthrow Eglon and bring peace. The theme of Moab drawing Israel into idolatry also reappears in the Book of Judges (10:6), which again is evidence of turning away from God and is evil in His sight. As we see in the Ten Commandments, God wanted the Israelites to be a people separated to Himself and serving Him exclusively (Exodus 20:3). Moab, however, is frequently seen as subtly fighting against that by encouraging God's people to adopt additional gods. Similarly, attacks on Christianity today may not be head-on and obvious, but more subtle, encouraging a "God-plus" mentality rather than faith in God alone.

And so we see Mahlon and Chilion marrying Moabite women. God had warned Israel that intermarrying with the nations they were to conquer would result in their being turned away from God and led into idolatry with other gods (Exodus 34:15-17). Although Moab strictly speaking wasn't included in this, the principle would have stood and certainly was assumed to be included in the guidance by those returning to Jerusalem following the Exile (Nehemiah 13:23). Christians today are similarly told not to marry unbelievers because of the difficulty in one partner being fully committed to God when the other serves other masters (2 Corinthians 6:14).

Things went from bad to worse for our family, as first Elimelech and then his sons die. We're not told why they died or anything more about what they did in Moab before their deaths. It's as if that isn't important; as if what they did and what happened to them didn't really matter. What matters and what is important are the events about to happen in the lives of Naomi, Ruth and Boaz whom we're yet to meet. The lives that are the focus of the story are those that are committed to God and through whom and for whom God is working to achieve His purposes of redemption. By this principle, is your life one that matters? Have you committed your life to Christ Jesus? Are you being used to achieve God's redemptive purposes?

When Naomi hears that circumstances had also changed in Bethlehem, she decides to return home. Initially both her daughters-in-law, Ruth and Orpah, follow her but then Naomi insists that they should remain in Moab and return to their families' homes. Did they remind Naomi of all she had lost?

Was she ashamed to bring Moabite daughters-in-law home to Bethlehem with her? Or was she genuinely concerned about their welfare, thinking that staying in Moab was the best option for them? We don't know. The narrator doesn't explain her motives, just quotes what she says.

Naomi argues that Ruth and Orpah would be better off returning to their families and finding husbands there. She makes reference to an Israelite law found in Deuteronomy 25:5-6 where Israelite men were to marry their brother's widows and provide for them, claiming this to be an improbable and impractical solution in their case and that they'd be better off looking elsewhere. We'll consider this law further when it resurfaces later in the book.

While it may look so far as if Naomi was wanting the best for her daughters-in-law, especially as she prayed that God would bless them for their kindness to her, verse 15 is troubling: "Look, your sister-in-law has gone back to her people and to her gods; return after your sister-in-law" (emphasis mine). Is Naomi really encouraging Ruth to return to idols? We can assume from what happens in verses 16-17 that Naomi and her family must have told Ruth and Orpah about God and their faith. We can assume that relationship with God was presented as a desirable thing. And yet here we have Naomi encouraging Ruth to return to Moabite gods! Do we give out mixed messages about God? Are we clear about who God is and the importance of following Him exclusively? Or do we muddy the waters and downplay the importance of what He says in the Bible?

Despite Naomi's urging, Ruth decides to follow her to Bethlehem. She makes an astounding commitment to Naomi:

> "Wherever you go, I will go;
> And wherever you lodge, I will lodge;
> Your people shall be my people,
> And your God, my God.
> Where you die, I will die,
> And there will I be buried.

> The LORD do so to me, and more also,
> If anything but death parts you and me" (vv. 16-17).

This passage, which is sometimes used in wedding ceremonies, to my mind holds an even greater significance and weight, given that it was made in a purely familial relationship. And yet, this seems far more than a commitment to Naomi, rather a declaration of Ruth's faith in God and her entering into the Covenant that God had made with Abraham. Note the parallel strands

"I... brought you out ... to give you this land" Genesis 15:7 "To your descendants I have given this land" Genesis 15:18 "I give to you ... all the land of Canaan, as an everlasting possession" Genesis 17:8	Focus on the land	"Wherever you go, I will go; and wherever you lodge, I will lodge" Ruth 1:16
"I will make you a great nation" Genesis 12:2 "Count the stars ... so shall your descendants be" Genesis 15:5 "I will bless you and ... multiply your descendants as the stars of the heaven and as the sand which is on the sea shore" Genesis 22:17	Focus on a people and nation	"Your people shall be my people" Ruth 1:16

| "… to be God to you and your descendants after you … and I will be their God" Genesis 17:7-8 | Focus on relationship with God | "and your God, my God" Ruth 1:16 |

Was Ruth's real commitment here to God rather than just to Naomi? Ruth obviously intended this commitment to last beyond Naomi's lifetime, as she mentions death and burial place. She wasn't following God and His ways merely on the surface, for Naomi's benefit, but was making it personal and real. Her actions in the chapters that follow certainly demonstrate a commitment to following God's laws and His way of doing things, rather than her own way. Can this be said of us? Is it evident from the way we live that we are followers of Christ?

Was Orpah wrong to return home? Once again, the Bible doesn't pass comment. On paper, it seems the easy and sensible decision – returning to family, safety and the known, rather than abandoning all for uncertainty and the unknown with Naomi. There was no guarantee of a home in Bethlehem, of a family, of meeting daily needs, and Naomi didn't seem overly welcoming, whereas at home she'd at least know there were loved ones and know the status quo. Sometimes we're presented with choices where neither option is right or wrong in and of itself. Are we willing, like Ruth, to step out in faith and move out of our comfort zone, trusting in God to provide? This may not mean leaving home, family and country, but adopting a mentality where faith enters all our decision-making. We don't hear what happened to Orpah. We don't know if she got a "happily ever after" or not. We do know, however, that Ruth was blessed for her step of faith (but that's a spoiler for future chapters!).

And so Naomi and Ruth arrive back in Bethlehem. The locals recognise Naomi and excitement is stirred. Naomi, however, puts a dampener on their excitement: "… the Almighty has dealt very bitterly with me. I went out full, and the LORD has brought me home again empty. Why do you call me Naomi, since the LORD has testified against me, and the Almighty has afflicted me?" (v. 21). A lot has happened to Naomi since she left Bethlehem, so much so that she refuses to be known any more in association with her old life as Naomi, meaning "pleasant". Instead, she insists on being called Mara, meaning "bitter" (cf. Exodus 15:23). Naomi claims a complete reversal in circumstances that this change in name symbolised. Yet her memory and accounting seem a little faulty here. Naomi claims that when she left Bethlehem, she was full and that now she is empty. Yes, she had lost her husband and sons while in Moab, but she seems to forget or ignore two key points. Firstly, it was famine that drove her family from Bethlehem, so they certainly weren't full physically and, chances are, they probably had experienced poverty and loss in Bethlehem prior to deciding to leave. Secondly, Ruth was with Naomi and had just made a massive commitment of dedication to her. How often our memories and accounting are similar to that of Naomi! When things are going badly, we often forget that our decisions played a part in creating the circumstances we're in and don't acknowledge the blessings that we do have and ultimately all that God has done for us. Or we blame God when things go wrong, while denying His existence or refusing to follow Him when things are going well.

How often it is that we need to become empty, like Naomi, before God starts to fill us! With regard to our salvation, we need to acknowledge, like Paul, that "in me ... nothing good dwells" (Romans 7:18) and that there's nothing we can do to earn salvation, before we will accept God's free gift and our need of Him. The writer to the Hebrews uses the analogy of a runner with baggage and burdens that need to be removed before they can run God's race effectively (Hebrews 12:1). Similarly, we often need to remove all the things that are clogging up our lives before we can be filled with the blessings God wants to pour into us. This emptying may not be pleasant at the time but is surely for our good.

Chapter 1 ends by informing us that Naomi and Ruth arrived in Bethlehem "at the beginning of barley harvest" (v. 22). Isn't it just like God to provide hope in the midst of tragedy? Barley was the first of the crops to be harvested, and so the whole of the harvest was still ahead. As we shall see in the following chapters, the harvest plays a huge part in the rest of the story. Our widows could have arrived after the harvest or during the sowing season, when they would have had to wait long months before the blessing could be claimed. Instead they arrive just in time to start claiming the harvest. Likewise, when we return to God and are saved, we receive a multitude of blessings immediately. We don't have to work to earn them or wait a probationary period. We don't arrive too late to find that all the blessings have been claimed by others before us, leaving none for us. So many of the promises of the Bible are ours the moment we become Christians.

As the first of the grain harvests, the start of the barley harvest would have been marked by the Feast of Firstfruits. Leviticus 23:9-14 is the main passage explaining what the Feast of Firstfruits was about. It was a festival the Israelites were told to celebrate once they entered the Promised Land. They were to bring the first sheaf of grain harvested and present it to the Lord. They were forbidden from eating of the harvest themselves until after this had been done, symbolising how God should be first in their lives and how all their blessings originate from God. Firstfruits came during the week-long Feast of Unleavened Bread, which began with the Passover. As such, God's work of salvation for the Israelites should have been fresh in the minds of Naomi and those around her at the time she returned to Bethlehem. Those closer to the time when this was written or from a Jewish background would more readily make this connection, though today's readers may not. The Israelites had been celebrating the salvation and freedom from Egypt which

God had provided, their pilgrimage in the wilderness, and God's faithfulness in bringing them into the land. And here were Ruth and Naomi, brought back from a foreign land of foreign gods into the land of promise in time to begin receiving the blessings God had planned for them!

On this side of the cross, we see Christ's death typified in the Passover (1 Corinthians 5:7), and His resurrection in the Firstfruits (1 Corinthians 15:20, 23). We then, like Ruth and Naomi, are living in the time between these spring festivals and the events represented by the autumn festivals at the end of the harvest, symbolising Christ's return and judgement of sin (I found Bryan Sheldon's book, "The Messiah and the Feasts of Israel", really interesting and understandable in expounding the feasts and their symbolism). In John 4:35, Jesus describes the world as "already white for harvest". Again, in Matthew 9:37 and Luke 10:2 Jesus describes the harvest as great or plentiful and in need of those to gather the harvest. Are we doing our part in this? Are we, like the disciples, going out and doing our part in reaping a harvest of souls for the Lord?

Points for further thought or action

- ❖ Is your testimony for God and the importance of what He says in His Word clear and consistent, or do things you say or do muddy the water and point to something else?
- ❖ When times are difficult, does your faith waver and result in bitterness towards God? How can this be minimised?
- ❖ God wants to bless us. How have you seen His blessing in your life at just the right time?

Chapter 2

Read the Book of Ruth and then reread chapter 2.

❖ Why does the chapter start with a parenthesis about Boaz being a relative of Elimelech? Why not wait until later in the chapter when we meet Boaz?

❖ What is gleaning all about? (see Deuteronomy 24:19-22)

❖ What does this chapter tell us about the characters of Ruth and Boaz?

❖ How has Naomi changed between the end of chapter 1 and the end of chapter 2?

❖ What does this chapter teach us about God?

Just as chapter 1 ends with a hint of hope to come, chapter 2 opens with another foretaste of hope: "There was a relative of Naomi's husband, a man of great wealth, of the family of Elimelech. His name was Boaz" (v. 1). In chapter 1 Naomi used the lack of any sons to marry Ruth as part of her argument as to why Ruth should return to Moab, and yet here we see that there still remained relatives of her husband's family who could keep the family name and inheritance, fulfilling the role of the kinsman. Not only was there hope of a kinsman, but he was wealthy, suggesting that he was more than capable of meeting the needs of our two widows. That he was "of the family of Elimelech" (v. 3) is repeated, as if to be doubly secure in the fact that there was one who could be called upon to fulfil the law's requirements. It is only after these details that we are told the man's name – Boaz. It's as if his name isn't really important. The main point is that he has the qualifications to meet the real needs of Naomi and Ruth. The story then quickly returns its focus to Ruth and Naomi in their current dilemma, but this first verse again provides clues as to how their crisis would be resolved.

When the Law was given to Israel prior to entering the land, provision was made for those who were less well off. This was not intended to excuse laziness, but to cater for those who through no fault of their own had come by hardship. The Israelites were to "remember that [they] were ... slave[s] in the land of Egypt" (Deuteronomy 24:22) and as such not to oppress those less fortunate. They were to provide means so that people could avoid selling themselves into slavery once more. During harvest, Israelite landowners were not to go back over land or trees to ensure that produce was not missed. They were deliberately to refrain from gathering crops at the edges of fields or return for what was left behind. This portion was to be left for "the stranger, the fatherless and the widow" (Deuteronomy 24:19, 21). In those days, foreigners, orphans and widows would have been among the most vulnerable of society and would have limited means of providing for themselves, so God instructed those who were better off to provide for them. These laws are outlined in Leviticus 19:9-10, 23:22 and Deuteronomy 24:19-22.

Deuteronomy 24:19 suggests that this law was also for the benefit of the landowners - "that the Lord your God may bless you in all the work of your hands". By leaving gleanings for the poor, landowners were forgoing the financial benefit that these crops could have been to them personally. Following God's law involved putting God and His commands above personal gain. Similar to presenting the Firstfruits to God, leaving gleanings symbolised a reliance on God to provide and an acknowledgement that all their blessings originated from Him.

God's instructions to care for those less fortunate are repeated in the Church context. In the days of the early church, believers shared their possessions so that "there were no needy persons among them" (Acts 4:34, NIV). 1 Timothy 5:3-16 provided detailed instructions as to how widows should be cared for and by whom. Those who had other means should use them and those who had families should be cared for by their families. Yet those who were faithful members of the church and had no other means of support should be supported by the church and not neglected. Similarly, James states that supporting orphans and widows is what is truly accepted by God as religious service rather than outward pretence (James 1:26-27). Likewise, Jesus chastised the Pharisees for their religious pretence and showy display rather than caring for family and those in need (Mark 7:9-13). God wants us to care for those around us, particularly those in the Church — to think of others' welfare rather than our own (Galatians 6:10).

And yet the Bible doesn't just tell us of a God who wants to meet our physical needs. Nor is the message of the Bible primarily about social justice. God knows that we all have a deeper need than food or shelter, or offspring to continue the family line.

He knows that the biggest problem each and every one of us has is sin. God's plan to deal with sin and meet our spiritual needs is what the Bible is all about. Right from the Fall, God promised a Deliverer who would defeat Satan and his control over us (Genesis 3:15). Right through the prophets we have glimpses of God's master plan and teasers, as it were, of what's to come. In the narrative of the Old Testament, we see pictures of what God is going to do to provide for us. We see the threads of God's plan of redemption being woven throughout the whole of the Old Testament. The Gospels then show God's plan coming together and being revealed in Jesus. God sent His Son, Jesus, to pay the death penalty that sin demands, so that by accepting this provision we can be saved and have our relationship with God restored. How truly great is our God!

To return to our chapter, Ruth lays claim to this provision by going to glean in the fields of Bethlehem. We see no sense of reluctance in Ruth to identify herself with those for whom the provision of gleaning was made – poor, fatherless, widows and foreigners. She accepted her place amongst the lowest of society in order to receive the blessing God had set apart for them. We too need to recognise our position and need as sinners before a just and holy God, and our need of His provision. As one new to Bethlehem and the people of Israel, Ruth first asks Naomi's permission to go and glean. Was she unsure of how things were done in Bethlehem? Was she seeking advice on the advisability of her plan or which fields would be best and most likely to give her a favourable response? Was she submitting to Naomi as head of the family in the absence of their husbands? We're not told, but we do see Naomi consenting to Ruth's proposition and, as the book goes on, we see Naomi taking more of an interest and active role in Ruth's future plans. Do we likewise seek advice and support from those older in the faith? Do we take an active interest and care for those less mature? This principle of seeking advice from those more experienced, and teaching those younger than oneself is applied by Paul to the women in the church in Titus 2:3-4 and should be foundational in our churches today.

In verse 3, Ruth begins gleaning and "it just so happened" (ICB) that she comes to the part of the field that belonged to Boaz ("her hap was to light upon..." ASV; "she chanced to light on ..." (Darby); "she happened to ..." NKJV, ESV; "as it happened" NLT; "as it turned out" NIV). The narrator makes it sound as if it was a fluke - purely by chance - that Ruth came to that particular field. And it probably was, from Ruth's perspective. We know from Naomi's questioning later in the chapter that Naomi hadn't directed Ruth to go to Boaz's field (or any other). And yet from the rest of the book it is plain that this was not just a chance occurrence but one planned by God for His greater purposes. Just as with Abraham's servant in Genesis 24:27 Ruth would be able to say "the LORD led me". How like the Good Shepherd of Psalm 23 to lead Ruth to pastures where her needs could be met and to guide her on to the path she should take to her redeemer. And, just in case we've forgotten, it is reiterated that Boaz "was of the family of Elimelech" (v. 3).

Boaz enters the story in person in verse 4 and the first thing he does is proclaim the blessing of God upon his workers: "The LORD be with you!" Boaz knows God to be a good God, and for His presence to be a blessing. How different this is to Naomi at the end of Chapter 1, who saw God as afflicting her, set against her and the cause of her emptiness. What do our words say about how we see God? Wouldn't it be good if we were known for speaking regularly about God and drawing His name into every situation? The workers respond in kind: "The LORD bless you!" While this may have been a common greeting and response, it may also paint a picture of the relationship between Boaz and his workers. If so, it is a picture of happy workplace relations and mutual respect and cooperation. Boaz was the kind of boss that his workers could readily seek God's blessing on – not grumbling at and badmouthing him but seeking his good. This positive picture of Boaz would fit with what we see of him in the rest of the book, including how he notices a stranger among the workers and seeks to find out who she is.

Boaz enquires of the servant in charge as to who this stranger may be. The servant tells him who she is and represents her positively as a hard worker who courteously asked permission to glean. While there are some obvious differences, this favourable report of action contrasts with that of the servants during the master's absence in the Parable of the Talents in Matthew 25:14-30. May we not be like that lazy servant who could not give his master a positive report of his work during the master's absence.

And so Boaz and Ruth meet. We don't hear whether it was love at first sight, whether their eyes met over the field of barley, or whether the wind rippled her hair … or any of the other romantic lines that normally accompany a love story. But that's because this isn't what the world would see as a typical love story. Love isn't even mentioned in the book. Yet the story is so patently about love, but not the fickle, changing, crazy love that fills whirlwind romances. This is a much deeper love that incorporates duty and commitment to others, and ultimately revolves around God. It is the love between redeemer and the redeemed, the love Christ shows for us. So we see Boaz graciously providing for Ruth, not just the gleanings commanded in the Law, but going above and beyond this. He encourages her to remain in his fields throughout the harvest, extends to her a place alongside his servant girls, offers protection from those who could harm her and provides refreshment from his water vessels and a place at his table (vv. 8-9,14). Not only this, he instructs his harvesters not to reproach her and to purposefully leave gleanings for her to collect (vv. 15-16). Ruth enters the field as a Moabitess – one who was of a despised race and excluded from the Israelite community (Deuteronomy 23:3) – and leaves it as a thoroughly accepted and adopted member of Boaz's harvest community, even being referred to as "my daughter" (v. 8). How many similarities this has to what Christ gives us as believers:

"my daughter"/ adoption as sons	Ephesians 1:5; Romans 8:19; Galatians 4:6
Encouraged to stay with his maidens/fellowship	Hebrews 10:25
Protection	1 Corinthians 10:13
Refreshment from thirst	John 7:37
A place at his table	John 6:35
Freedom from reproach	Romans 8:33, 34
Liberal giving	Romans 8:32; Ephesians 1:3, 7-8; James 1:5

And that's just naming a few! Reading Romans 8 and Ephesians 1 reveals so many of the blessings we have in Christ simply by being Christians. How great is our God! Like Ruth we can bow in worship and exclaim: "Why have I found favour in your eyes, that you should take notice of me …?" cf. Psalm 8:4; 2 Samuel 9:8. While in Ruth's case it could be said that her character and kindness to Naomi had prompted Boaz's kindness, in our case it couldn't be further from the truth. Paul, in Romans 7:18, states that "in me (that is, in my flesh) nothing good dwells". In addition, Jeremiah tells us:

> "The heart is deceitful above all things,
> And desperately wicked" (Jeremiah 17:9).

There is nothing in any of us deserving of God's grace and yet He still chooses to bestow it upon us. It is truly by grace that we are saved (Ephesians 2:8), not as a result of who we are or of what we can achieve. All that is required of us is that, like Ruth, we have faith in God to save us – that we find refuge under His wings.

In verse 11, Boaz informs Ruth that he is aware of all that she has done for Naomi and that she has turned to the LORD as her God. This is more than the report provided by his servant. The news was out in Bethlehem and had made its way to Boaz's ears. We don't hear that Ruth had been publicising this information. Ruth didn't need to explain to Boaz why she was there or what she had done. Naomi may have been telling others about Ruth but we don't see that in her commentary of what had happened in Moab in the end of Chapter 1. How much of this information was assumed or inferred from what was or wasn't said and from the locals' observation? Our testimonies are clearly meant to be more than merely the words we say. How good it would be if, like Ruth, those around us would find cause for praise in us before we speak a word! In 1 Peter 3:1-4 Peter exhorts wives to show godly conduct so that "without a word" their husbands would see the transformation Christ makes in a life and may be saved too. Similarly, in 1 Peter 2:12-15, it is by doing good, not by clever or comprehensive argument, that we are to "silence the ignorance of foolish men" and that our conduct may cause unbelievers to glorify God. How clear is the Gospel that my life preaches? It was because of Ruth's kindness to her mother-in-law that Boaz was praising her. She could have been like Orpah and returned to Moab or she could have left Naomi once they arrived in Bethlehem, but then she wouldn't have received Boaz's favour. Ruth didn't set out to earn Boaz's favour and she didn't show kindness to Naomi intending to be rewarded for it, and yet that was the outcome. This parallels Jesus' teaching in Matthew 25:34-40, where the king rewards those who served "the least of these" as if they had done it for Him, and in Matthew 10:40-42 where individuals are blessed for what they do for Christ's servants.

During the working day, Boaz and his harvesters take time out to share a meal, and Ruth is invited to join them. This simple meal, covered in only one verse, is a beautiful reminder of the supper Jesus shared with His disciples (Matthew 26:17-30; Mark 14:12-26; Luke 22:14-23). Both Ruth and the disciples were invited to come and to eat; both meals involved bread and a form of wine; both situations had a communal aspect of passing food to one another. The chapter doesn't say, but there is the impression that this communal mealtime wasn't a one-off occasion but something that would have been done regularly (daily), even as we are encouraged to replicate regularly the Lord's Supper - "as often as you eat this bread and drink this cup" - in remembrance of Him (1 Corinthians 11:26, emphasis mine).

After a day of gleaning, Ruth proceeded to beat out what she had gathered, to separate that which was good for food from the rest of the plant. Do I do this after having received teaching on God's Word? Am I like the Bereans in Acts 17:11, who took the teaching of Paul and measured it against the Scriptures to determine its validity? Am I willing to dig deep and put in the extra work to gain the real blessing? Not only this, but Ruth also brought back some of the food she had been given to share with Naomi. When we learn something from – are fed by – the Word, do we take it home and share it with others? The exact amount that Ruth took home – "about an ephah of barley" (v. 17) – is converted by scholars differently, but may be about 22 litres. In the wilderness, the Israelites were to gather manna daily and the amount they were to collect was an omer, or tenth of an ephah, per person per day. Thus, one ephah of manna was enough for two people for five days. While the volume of manna may not equate directly to the volume of barley, it is evident that Ruth had gathered a lot and potentially enough to last the two widows most of the week. The abundance of Ruth's gleaning is further supported by Naomi's surprise at how much it was, enough to invoke a blessing on whoever was behind the bounty.

It is only upon learning that Boaz had been behind Ruth's abundance that Naomi sees the hand of God at work for blessing once more in her life. We see her receiving a glimmer of hope that all may not be lost and that she may not be as empty as she first supposed. Naomi realised that it is Boaz's connection to the family that has caused him to be so generous so far, and has the hope that this signifies a greater care for them that will result in his being their kinsman-redeemer.

Points for further thought and action

❖ What role does the Church play in responding to God's children who are in need? How are you/could you be part of that?

❖ Do you seek advice from more mature Christians? Do you take an active interest in those who are younger/weaker in faith?

❖ In what ways is God blessing you at the moment? Do you actively look for His blessings in your life, or is your focus elsewhere?

Chapter 3

Read the Book of Ruth and then reread chapter 3.

❖ What was the role of the kinsman according to the Mosaic Law? (see Leviticus 25:25; Deuteronomy 25:5-10)

❖ Boaz describes Ruth's kindness in this scene as greater than that she had shown earlier. What does he mean?

❖ Boaz informs Ruth of a nearer kinsman and then says that it would be good if the other would marry her – why is this? Why doesn't Boaz just say "yes"?

❖ What does this chapter teach us about God?

In chapter 2 we saw how Ruth and Naomi's immediate need for food was met and how the laws God instituted in the Torah provided a system through which this could be accomplished and safeguarded. In chapter 3 and 4, we'll see how the widows' longer-term needs for security and a home will be met. Once again, God ensured that laws existed to facilitate this.

Remember when Naomi was encouraging Ruth and Orpah to return to the homes of their mothers and to seek husbands in Moab. Do you recall the law that she made reference to when she lamented that she was too old to have more sons and that her daughters-in-law would have to wait too long in any case before the sons would be of a marriageable age? This law, the law regarding **levirate marriage**, is found in Deuteronomy 25:5-10 and states that a man should marry his brother's childless widow in order to preserve the family name by raising up an heir for the deceased brother. Instructions are given as to what should be done if the surviving brother declines. The refusal should be a matter of public concern; the elders should challenge the man and, in the event of his still declining, it would result in public shaming. The surviving brother had other duties in Israelite society. Referred to in Hebrew as the "Go'el", he could redeem property or persons that had been sold during times of hardship (Leviticus 25:25). He was the one to whom restoration could be paid where a relative had been wronged (Numbers 5:5-8); the one who was to be the avenger of blood when a relative was murdered (Numbers 35:9-30). While it's fairly clear that the latter two scenarios were not relevant in Naomi and Ruth's story, either or both of the first two could have been in Naomi's mind as she points out to Ruth that Boaz was their close relative – their Go'el.

And so Naomi sets out her plan for gaining security for Ruth. She was to wash and get dressed up ready to go to Boaz where he was known to be spending the night on the threshing floor. She was to wait until privacy would be assured and then lie down at Boaz's feet after having uncovered them, probably so that the cold on his feet would wake him. Does this sound like a wise plan to you? Brazen maybe, or full of scope to go wrong. Yet Naomi, who by now evidently has Ruth's best-interests at heart, is heard outlining this plan to Ruth. Given what we know of the morality of the times found in Judges, and the reputation of the Moabites, it speaks volumes about the characters of Boaz and Ruth that Naomi would suggest such a venture. Maybe part of the reason why this incident happens at the "end of barley harvest and wheat harvest" (2:23) is that enough time has passed to reassure all the townspeople and Boaz of Ruth's character – they all knew she was a virtuous woman (v. 11) – so there was less chance of Ruth's actions being misconstrued. Naomi would also have the reassurance of insight into Boaz's character and that he also was virtuous (2:1). While the Hebrew word is translated as "wealth" or "wealthy" in 2:1 and elsewhere (e.g. Genesis 34:29; Deuteronomy 8:17; 2 Kings 15:20), the same Hebrew word is translated "virtuous" when describing Ruth and "valour" when describing David (their descendant) in 1 Samuel 16:18. I don't think it is a coincidence that the same word is used to describe both Boaz and Ruth in this book (and also used of David), highlighting how both had characters suited to and complementing each other. The same word is also used of the woman in Proverbs 31:10 which, as discussed in the introduction, immediately precedes the Book of Ruth in some Hebrew collections, as if Ruth is intended as an example of the ideal found in Proverbs 31. (As an aside, the word "wealthy" adds to the second part of Proverbs 31:10 – "her worth is far above rubies" – stressing that wealth of character is far greater than earthly wealth.) And so, in the midst of general corruption, immorality and autonomy, we see the characters of Ruth and Boaz shining brightly with virtue and moral uprightness, or moral wealth. Christians are told to live as lights in the darkness of the world around them (Matthew 5:16; Philippians 2:15). When those with whom I have regular contact look at me, do they see that light? Am I, like Ruth, known as a "virtuous woman", to be "blameless and harmless … without fault in the midst of a crooked and perverse generation" (Philippians 2:15)? What do I need to do to make this a reality? What about you?

Naomi ends her instructions to Ruth with the assurance that "he will tell you what you should do" (v. 4). While it would naturally flow that the "he" of this refers to Boaz, some have seen enough ambiguity in it to suggest that Naomi may have been referring to God. Whether intended or not, the guidance to wait and listen for the voice of the Lord to guide us is excellent advice. Is it my habit of life to listen for His direction or to take things into my own hands and seek to keep a tight grip on the reins? Mary provides similar but not identical advice to the servants in Cana – "whatever He says to you, do it." (John 2:5). In verse 5, we see Ruth's response, affirming that she will follow Naomi's words to the letter. And just in case we missed it, not only does verse 6 inform us that Ruth "did according to all that her mother-in-law instructed her" but verse 7 reiterates how Ruth followed Naomi's advice. No "ifs". No "buts". No "are you sure?" No "you want me to do what?" Instead, Ruth readily agrees to follow advice and proves, by following through on her promise, that hers was not an empty acquiescence. How good it would be if we all accepted these two pieces of advice – to listen for His guidance and then to do it – into our daily lives, always having them at the forefront of our minds.

Having followed Naomi's guidance, Ruth is found on the threshing floor at Boaz's feet in the middle of the night. And it's here that we have Ruth making her request to Boaz: "Take your maidservant under your wing" (v. 9) or as "I am your servant ... spread the corner of your garment over me" (NIV). Now this may not sound like a marriage proposal to us today, but the same imagery is used in Ezekiel 16:8. There, the LORD speaks of Jerusalem as a woman whom He has nurtured from childhood into womanhood. As she reaches the "time of love", the LORD is seen to "spread [His] wing over [her] ... and [she] became [His]", depicting marriage between God and Israel.

The metaphor of wings also harks back to chapter 2:12 where Boaz praised Ruth for finding refuge under God's wings. The Psalms speak of the "shadow of [God's] wings" as being a place of refuge, safety and shelter (Psalm 17:8; 36:7; 57:1; 61:4; 91:4). It is a place where we can find joy (Psalm 63:7) and a place of healing (Malachi 4:2). Jesus also adopts the metaphor when He laments over Jerusalem and their rejection of Him (Luke 13:34). He states that He would have gathered them "as a hen gathers her brood under her wings". What a lovely picture of safety, warmth and comfort, all of which we can find in Him! Not long ago, I was at a children's farm and actually saw this happening. All the little chicks huddled under their mother where they were safe from toddlers' attention. What struck me, above the benefits to the individual chicks, was how many chicks the hen actually managed to fit under her wings! As the chicks began to emerge and the hen moved her wings, more chicks appeared than I had expected would fit there. There's room for all under the wings of our mighty Saviour. Have you come for refuge under the wings of our Kinsman-Redeemer?

In verse 10, Boaz blesses Ruth: "Blessed are you of the LORD, my daughter! For you have shown more kindness at the end than at the beginning, in that you did not go after young men, whether poor or rich." This blessing parallels that in chapter 2, where Boaz blessed Ruth, praising her for her dedication and kindness to Naomi. At that point Boaz was impressed by Ruth's choice to follow Naomi and provide for her rather than returning to Moab and all that was familiar. He knew of her commitment to follow "the LORD God of Israel" (2:12) and her trust that He would provide. Now Boaz claims that Ruth's current kindness in seeking marriage to him was more than all that had gone before. He recognised that Ruth was going above and beyond what the Law, strictly speaking, called for in levirate marriage (more about this in the next chapter). Ruth could have chosen to marry a Moabite. She could have chosen someone else in Israel. And yet she chose Boaz. Ruth chose the man who could fulfil the spirit of the Law and raise up an heir for Naomi and carry on the family line of the deceased. She chose to set aside her list of 'top-10-characteristics-to-look-for-in-Mr-Right' and focus instead on the one who would be the source of blessing for Naomi. Ruth's kindness didn't stop in accompanying Naomi and supporting her, but it extended to restoring that which had been lost; it extended to restoration and revival. Boaz recognised this and praised her for it. But he didn't stop there: he promised to honour her desire and request. He would gladly take up his role as a kinsman and marry her - but there was a snag. There was a closer relative who had a prior legal claim. This relative should be offered the chance to step up first, with Boaz waiting in the wings in case the other declined.

Why did Boaz think it would be "good" (v.13) if the other kinsman stepped up to the plate? Didn't Boaz want to marry Ruth? Why would he bring up an obstacle and then, of all things, say that that would be better? I think it speaks volumes about Boaz's character and his faithfulness to God's law. Yes, Boaz wanted to be the kinsman-redeemer and marry Ruth, but more important to him was following God's law. He wouldn't prioritise his desires over God's. This is how it should be for us too. It may be that we have ideas of how life should be – castles in the air that we've been constructing since childhood, where we would have the perfect job, family, friends and lifestyle. They may all be legitimate and good plans, but if they're not God's plans they're the wrong plans! That's not to say that we won't get the dreams we've been nurturing – Boaz did get to marry Ruth – but it should be God's way and God's timing that we follow. Consequently, Boaz had to defer to the closer kinsman. If the other kinsman did his duty, that would be a good thing because God's law was being followed Ruth would be protected and cared for and an heir would be raised up for Mahlon. All of this would have testified to God's provision and loving-kindness found in the Law and would have brought glory to God. Thankfully for Boaz, God's plan for Ruth involved him

— but more of that in the next chapter. For now, all we need to know is that Boaz was willing to meet Ruth's needs if the other kinsman wouldn't, and that Boaz was planning on sorting it all out without delay. No hesitating! No checking out the other relative's position first, waiting for the opportune moment or until he had crafted a killer argument for why the other relative should step aside. No, Boaz just takes the earliest opportunity to secure Ruth's future.

Come morning, Boaz rises early to send Ruth on her way before it was light enough for anyone to be recognised. Even then he was thinking of her reputation. Was he also thinking of the closer relative's claim and the effect a scandal, even if unfounded, could have on the situation? He does, however, take the time to provide for Ruth before she goes home. The exact amount of barley given is not clear – the "ephahs" (NKJV) isn't in the original text. Some see six measures as one measure short of perfection (seven in the Bible being seen as the number of perfection). They would suggest that while the other relation was in the picture, Boaz was unable to perfectly provide for Ruth, but that this was a promise of what was yet to come. Whether or not this is the case, we can assume that Ruth took home a good supply of barley.

Like Boaz, when we come to God as our Kinsman-Redeemer, He doesn't send us away empty-handed. We have been given "every spiritual blessing in the heavenly places in Christ" (Ephesians 1:3). Just as Ruth received the six measures of barley as a promise of what was to come, even so we have been given the Holy Spirit as a guarantee of the inheritance we have in the Lord Jesus (2 Corinthians 1:22; 5:5; Ephesians 1:13-14). Do we recognise all that God is giving us? Do we come to Him expecting more? After all, He's promised to give good things to those who ask (Matthew 7:11). We have a bountiful God who delights to give! Are we ready to receive His blessing?

"Then she told her all that the man had done for her" (v.16). Ruth must have been so desperate to tell her news. Things were starting to look good, really good, and Ruth wanted to share that good news and the hope for the future with her mother-in-law. As Christians, we have the best news, the Gospel, and the best hope for the future. Are we as keen as Ruth to tell others all that He has done for us? Or do we let fear or embarrassment, or "not wanting to impose our beliefs on others", or anything else, stop us from telling them the good news? When the lepers discovered that the Syrian army had fled, they soon realised that they would be in error if they kept silent. "We are not doing right. This day is a day of good news, and we remain silent … let us go and tell the king's household" (2 Kings 7:9). We too are living in a day of good news – the best news. Let us not keep silent. Let us go and tell those around us the good news of Christ's death and resurrection, which have made a way back to God in order to receive forgiveness of sins.

The chapter closes with Naomi providing another piece of advice to Ruth: "Sit still, my daughter, until you know how the matter will turn out; for the man will not rest until he has concluded the matter this day" (v. 18). Naomi is telling Ruth to wait patiently and trust in the man who holds her future in his hands. What good advice this is for us today! We also can trust the One who is our Redeemer. Once we've come to Him, we don't need to keep working and looking for ways to earn our salvation. Our salvation is based on what He has done, not on our works (Ephesians 2:8-9). Like Ruth, we can wait patiently for His return, knowing that He has done all that is required to make our redemption sure. We can also apply this lesson to our prayer lives. Once we've made our requests known to God, we don't have to worry about them and seek alternative solutions as though everything depends on us. Instead we can trust Him, that He knows what's best for us and is powerful enough to accomplish His purposes.

Points for further thought and action

❖ Ruth and Boaz's characters stand out in contrast to the times in which they lived, showing that they were following God. How does your life stand out as one who is following God? Do people know you're a Christian by how you live?

❖ To what extent do the two pieces of advice – "He will tell you what to do" and "Do whatever He tells you" – feature in your life and decision-making?

❖ God's plans are sometimes different from our plans. To what extent are you willing to follow His plans? Are there any non-negotiables in your plans, things you wouldn't give up if He asked you to?

❖ Do you trust God with your salvation or seek to earn it for yourself? Do you trust Him with your prayer requests?

Chapter 4

Read the Book of Ruth and then reread chapter 4.

❖ Why did Boaz go to the town gates? What role did the gates have in society at that time? (see Genesis 23:18; 34:20-21; Deuteronomy 21:19; 22:15, 24; 25:7; Joshua 20:4)

❖ What do the Mosaic laws Boaz is referring to involve? (see Leviticus 25:23-28; Deuteronomy 25:5-10)

❖ Why are Rachel, Leah and Tamar mentioned by the elders of the town? (see Genesis 29-30, 38 for their stories)

❖ In what ways has the story come full-circle for Naomi?

❖ What does this chapter teach us about God?

Chapter 4 opens with Boaz going "up to the gate" (v. 1). Now considering that we know Boaz was about to sort out the legalities relating to marrying Ruth, this may seem strange to us today – why didn't he just go round to the relative's house or find a local lawyer? In reality, that's what he did. In those days, the elders of the city would gather at the town gates to conduct business and deal with legal cases – similar to town hall business or a magistrates' court today. The town gates are where Abraham became legal owner of the burial ground near Mamre where he would bury Sarah (Genesis 23:18) and where Hamor and Shechem relayed the proposed marriage contract between Shechem and Dinah to the citizens of the town (Genesis 34:20-21). In the Law, the Israelites were instructed to take to the elders gathered at the gate: cases of rebellious children (Deuteronomy 21:19), marriage violations (Deuteronomy 22:15, 23-24), refusal to follow the law of levirate marriage (Deuteronomy 25:7), and manslaughter (Joshua 20:4). Both Lot and Job in their times were elders who sat at their town's gates (Genesis 19:1; Job 29:7). Boaz is therefore following the precedent of Abraham and Hamor in going to the town gates for business involving a land transaction and a marriage proposal.

Once at the gates, Boaz summons the nearer-kinsman to join him: "Come aside, friend, sit down here" (v. 1). "Friend" is probably too positive a translation. The term used, meaning "Such-and-such" or "So-and-so", is used when a name is to be hidden or not spoken aloud (cf. 1 Samuel 21:2). We can be sure that Boaz knew his name since he was a close relative. Why then do we not learn the name of the nearer-kinsman? It could be that the narrator was being kind to the unnamed man by not naming him in a context that doesn't portray him in a positive light. It could be that, as the story was verbally handed down and retold across generations until it was written down, the detail of his name was lost since it isn't relevant to the story. Yet it could also be intended that way, to highlight how insignificant this man's role was in the story (similar to earlier comments about the lack of details on Mahlon and Chilion) and to draw and fix readers' attention on those characters who are named and around which the story revolved – on Naomi, Ruth and Boaz.

Boaz wants to make sure that the business is dealt with publicly and openly, so that there will be no cause for doubt – potentially another reason for dealing with this in the town gates rather than in the home. As such, he invites "ten men of the elders of the city" (v. 2) to join him as witnesses to his legal affairs. It is only then that he makes known his request to the nearer-relative.

Boaz presents the case: brother Elimelech's land had ended up in need of redemption. Would the nearer-relative buy it? If he wouldn't, then Boaz was keen to buy it himself as the next in line. Only after the nearer-relative claimed he would buy the land did Boaz bring up the issue of marrying Ruth and raising up an heir for Mahlon. Why did Boaz deal with the issues in this order? And why not raise both issues together at the outset rather than linking them after an initial agreement to buy the land? Maybe Boaz, knowing the kinsman well enough, was drawing out his motives. He would gladly buy the land, which could be profitable for him and enlarge his own estate, but when it came to Ruth and raising another man's heir and putting his own inheritance in jeopardy, that was another matter entirely. Was he happy to fulfil the law as long as it profited him but less comfortable when it disadvantaged him, even though benefiting others? We don't know and the Bible doesn't say. Was Boaz dealing with the law that was definitely applicable, before bringing in the one that may be tenuous or disputable?

Now there are a couple of Mosaic laws at play in this chapter, that have been interwoven. As neither law plays a major part in our lives today, what they actually involved is likely to be a bit sketchy for us, so let's have a closer look at each of them.

	Leviticus 25:23-28: **Redemption of Property**	**Deuteronomy 25:5-10** **Levirate Marriage**
Sphere of reference	Sale of land	Childless widows
Purpose of law	To keep the land within the family to whom God allotted it	To maintain the family line and name. Also, a means of providing for the widow's welfare
Relation to Abrahamic covenant	Promise of the land as an everlasting possession	Promise of descendants and a nation. Promise of the line through which the Messiah would come
Problem it deals with	Land sold by an Israelite as a result of poverty	Death of a husband before a son and heir was born – potential ending of a family line
Prospective redeemer	Nearest relative Failing such, the man who sold the land is able to redeem it, should circumstances change and allow it	The deceased's brother
Lack of a willing/ able redeemer	Land to be returned during the Year of Jubilee (every 50 years)	Widow to go to the elders at the town gates who would question the brother. If he was adamant that he would not marry her, then she was to remove his sandal and spit in his face. The man would then be stigmatised by the congregation for refusing to fulfil his duty.

Strictly speaking, some commentators agree that the Law did not require either man to marry Ruth. The word used in the original Hebrew of Deuteronomy 25 (*yabam*) refers to 'brother-in-law' or 'husband's brother' rather than the meaning of the word used in Leviticus 25 (*ach*), which is a broader term for 'brother' that can extend to any relative or even wider. So why did Boaz potentially complicate matters by merging the two laws together and even making mention of the Deuteronomy law? If the other relative had been Chilion, then yes, the law would definitely apply to him as Mahlon's brother. But we know that Naomi's sons were both dead so this law shouldn't apply. This would certainly fit Naomi's comments in chapter 1 that imply that the levirate law was inapplicable since she had no surviving sons. It may be that Boaz was referring to the spirit rather than the letter of the law – the intention that the widow would be cared for and an heir raised up for the deceased, even if it wasn't a direct brother who fulfilled it. Or it may be that common custom at the time interpreted the law in that way. Alternatively, marrying Ruth may have been a stipulation that Naomi set out on purchasing the land. Whichever way, the nearer-kinsman didn't protest against the two laws being linked together (and I get the impression that if he could have got away with taking the land without marrying Ruth, he would have done).

Fearing for his own inheritance and the implications for this of having children through Ruth, the nearer-relative stepped aside. The way was cleared for Boaz to claim land and bride. To seal the deal, a local custom was enacted: "one man took off his sandal and gave it to the other, and this was a confirmation in Israel" (v. 7). Boaz wanted no doubt and no room for anyone to question his right to act as kinsman-redeemer. We can understand that – it's no different to signing a contract today – but what is taking the other man's shoe all about?

Some suggest that this links in with the Deuteronomy law where the widow was to take off a sandal of the brother-in-law who refused to marry her, claiming that this is also why the other relative is not named (Deuteronomy 25:9-10). But this doesn't really fit, if that law didn't apply. Besides, in the story of Ruth it's the man removing his sandal and giving it to Boaz, not Ruth removing it from him. Also, there's no mention of spitting in his face – of publicly shaming him: Ruth wasn't even there at the town gates; she was back at home with Naomi (3:18). It's more likely that this shoe-giving was linked with the exchange of the land: verse 7 even states that the custom was "concerning redeeming and exchanging". In the Old Testament there is a strong link between where one walks and God's giving of the land to that one as a possession. In Genesis 13:17 Abraham is told to wander throughout the land of Canaan, symbolically laying claim to the whole land; Caleb is gifted "the land where [his] foot has trodden" as an inheritance because of his faithfulness (Joshua 14:9); and the promise to Abraham is reiterated to the Israelites as they prepared to enter the Promised Land (Deuteronomy 11:22-25). It appears that a custom of sandal-exchange developed to symbolise how it would not be the current holder's feet that would walk on and claim the land.

Just in case the elders had missed what was going on, Boaz clearly states what had just transpired: he had purchased all that had belonged to Elimelech, Mahlon and Chilion and had betrothed himself to Ruth with the intention of raising up an heir for Mahlon. The elders bore witness to this and gave their blessing to Boaz: "The LORD make the woman who is coming to your house like Rachel and Leah, the two who built the house of Israel; and may you prosper in Ephrathah and be famous in Bethlehem. May your house be like the house of Perez, whom Tamar bore to Judah, because of the offspring which the LORD will give you from this young woman." (vv. 11-12). Now it's easy to get the gist of what the elders are saying – that they hope Boaz and Ruth's family will be prosperous and well known – but why do they use the analogies of Rachel, Leah and Tamar? For those who know much of the stories of these women, it may seem strange that they were used as positive examples of family life. Why didn't the elders choose different characters, ones with unquestionable integrity? Let's have a recap on the histories of these women.

When Jacob fled from the wrath of his brother Esau after tricking him out of their father's blessing, he went to stay with his uncle, Laban. There he fell in love with his cousin, Rachel, and served Laban for seven years to gain her hand in marriage. On the wedding night, Laban switched Rachel for her sister, Leah, only later giving Rachel to Jacob as a wife (for another seven years of service), as told in Genesis 29. The end of Genesis 29 and the first half of chapter 30 tell of the ensuing rivalry between the sisters as they compete for Jacob's attention, using their children and maidservants as means of gaining favour. For Rachel, the drive to have children led to her death in childbirth (Genesis 35:16-20). It's a tale of bitterness, jealousy and rivalry with little, if any, focus on seeking God's will or following His ways. And yet this is the family set-up from which the twelve tribes of Israel came! God used these women to build His chosen people and as the impetus for expanding a family into a nation. Surely it's this concept of founding a nation and fruitfulness to which the elders are referring in their blessing of Boaz and Ruth.

Tamar and her history, on the other hand, is probably one that you wouldn't want to be broadcast – one of those family skeletons in the cupboard that the tribe all know about but want to ignore and remove themselves from as much as possible. Genesis 38 breaks the flow of Joseph's storyline to tell about Judah and Tamar. Judah had three sons: Er, Onan and Shelah. He arranged for the marriage of his eldest son to Tamar. However, because of Er's wickedness, "the Lord killed him" (Genesis 38:7). In accordance with levirate custom (this was before the law was given by Moses: it would appear that the custom predates the Law), Judah arranged for Onan to marry Tamar so that he could "raise up an heir to [his] brother" (v. 8). Onan had other thoughts. He didn't want to have children with Tamar because he knew that the child would be seen as his brother's. As such he made efforts to ensure Tamar wouldn't become pregnant. As a result of this, "the LORD ... killed him also" (v. 10). Judah is reluctant to lose his third and final son to the twice-widowed Tamar so plays for time, quoting Shelah's youth as an excuse for delaying their marriage. Years later, realising that Judah had no intention of arranging the third marriage, Tamar took matters into her own hands. Disguising herself as a shrine prostitute, she slept with Judah and became pregnant with his child. When Judah realises that he's been caught out and what's happened, he claims that Tamar had actually been "more righteous" than he since she was following the levirate custom in her own way while he was refusing to do so (Genesis 38:14, 26). Perez, along with his twin Zerah, was born of this union. Boaz, and it is thought many of the other Bethlehemites at the time, was a direct descendant of Perez.

But what's so positive about this story that would cause the Bethlehemites to use it as a blessing, even if Perez was their ancestor? Let's have a look at the similarities and differences between the two situations:

Tamar and Judah	Ruth and Boaz
Tamar was a Gentile, Judah an Israelite	Ruth was a Gentile, Boaz an Israelite
Involved levirate marriage principles (although extended beyond direct brother-in-law)	Involved levirate marriage principles (although extended beyond direct brother-in-law)
Judah refused to follow the levirate custom	Boaz was willing to follow the levirate custom
Tamar took things into her own hands to produce an heir	Ruth trusted in God (and Boaz and Naomi) to work things out at the right time

Tamar described as righteous by Judah for her desire to perpetuate the family name	Ruth praised by Boaz as virtuous and for her kindness in her desire to perpetuate the family name

I think that what the elders were expressing was an admiration for following the principles of levirate marriage, the praiseworthiness of Ruth in seeking this and the blessing of incorporating a Gentile into the household of faith as a result of it. The benefit of being on this side of the cross also enables us to look back and see how the actions of both women resulted in their being included in the family tree of the Messiah (Matthew 1). For a people who had such a focus on the promise of One who would be a blessing to many nations and who would fulfil the prophecy in Genesis 3:15, this would have been a blessing indeed.

"The LORD gave her conception, and she bore a son" (v. 13). Isn't it beautiful how this is phrased? Not just that Ruth has a son, but that God is the cause of it, that God sees fit to bless them with a son. The Bible teaches that all children are a gift from God (Psalm 127:3; Isaiah 8:18). However, throughout the Old Testament we see it specifically mentioned that God gave conception to certain women. God "did for Sarah as He had spoken. For Sarah conceived and bore Abraham a son" (Genesis 21:1-2); the "LORD granted [Isaac's] plea, and Rebekah his wife conceived" (Genesis 25:21); God "opened [Leah's] womb" when He saw she was unloved by Jacob (Genesis 29:31 and again in 30:17); He "remembered Rachel ... and opened her womb" (Genesis 30:22); Manoah's barren wife was visited by the Angel of the LORD and informed that she would have a son (Judges 13:3); barren Hannah prayed for a son and "the LORD ... granted [her] petition" (1 Samuel 1:27). Similarly, Luke 1 tells of how barren, aged Elizabeth, and virgin Mary conceived following announcements by angels that this is what God was going to do for them. In each of these instances, sons are born whom God then uses mightily for His purposes. Likewise,

Ruth's son, Obed, was to be the grandfather of David, the great King of Israel, a fact which this closing chapter of Ruth refers to twice (vv. 17, 22).

But before those genealogies are recorded, we see the women of Bethlehem bless Naomi. Here it is Obed, the son of Ruth and Boaz, who is referred to as the "close relative" and "restorer of life" (vv. 14-15). Naomi's story starts with grief, hunger, loss and emptiness, and ends with restoration, life, fullness, joy and love. The story has come full circle. Yet, arguably, more than a return to baseline has occurred. Naomi now has a grandson and the hope for future generations that that entails. Not only is the famine over, but she now has a wealthy landowner providing for her needs. And she has Ruth, whose love and loyalty have been abundantly proven since we met her in chapter 1 and who even the town's people recognise as "better than seven sons" (v. 15). In a culture where sons were an essential attribute, that speaks volumes. Add to that how seven in the Bible is often seen as the number of perfection, for Ruth to be better than the perfect number of sons is abundant praise. Isn't this how it is with God? His blessings don't just get us back to a neutral baseline when our sins are forgiven. Instead He has superabundantly blessed us "with every spiritual blessing in the heavenly places" (Ephesians 1:3). How great and generous is our God!

Points for further thought and action

❖ The other kinsman feared for his own inheritance if he took on Ruth and the land. Does fear ever stop you from doing what God asks?

❖ The chapter states that God enabled Ruth to have a son. Do you see the good things in your life as gifts from God?

❖ God has blessed us "with every spiritual blessing in the heavenly places" (Ephesians 1:3). That is true, regardless of external circumstances. Are you delighting in the abundant blessings of God?

How does the Book of Ruth point to Jesus?

Read the Book of Ruth.

❖ What themes have you seen emerging throughout the Book of Ruth that point to the big picture of God's plan?

❖ How does what the Book of Ruth teaches us about God fit into the Bible as a whole?

❖ How do the lessons we've learnt from the book point to Jesus?

The Book of Ruth is more than just a story of two widows in ancient Israel. It's about more than their journey from emptiness to fullness. The whole Bible, the Book of Ruth included, is Jesus' story. If we view the Bible as a tapestry, we can see the different coloured threads running from Genesis to Revelation, some colours more prominent than others, some rising to the forefront for a time before returning to the background. Let's have a look at some of the whole-Bible themes that are prominent in the Book of Ruth and see how this short book points us to Jesus.

Redemption

Perhaps the biggest theme of the whole Bible is God's plan of redemption. We see it emerging right after the Fall with God's promise that one day He would send a Man who would defeat Satan and restore people from the brokenness caused by sin (Genesis 3:15). We see this storyline develop through the Old Testament as time after time someone is raised up temporarily to save God's people and promises are made of the Coming One who would permanently and fully save His people. We see how God's plan came to fruition in the life, death and resurrection of Jesus. And we see how that redemption affects us now and gives promises of greater things to come in the rest of the New Testament. Yet nowhere in the Bible is the kinsman-redeemer aspect portrayed so clearly as in the Book of Ruth.

A kinsman-redeemer was needed in cases where persons or property had been sold in times of poverty, to obtain vengeance for murder and to restore a dead family-line. In order to qualify as a kinsman-redeemer, one had to be a close relative of the one in need, and be both able and willing to help.

As fallen mankind, we have in effect been sold into slavery to sin with no way of paying the debt we owe to redeem ourselves. Sin brought spiritual death into the world, in effect murdering the relationship between God and mankind; and our family-line through Adam can be seen as dead and dying, to be restored only through new birth and new life. Our need for a Kinsman-Redeemer to free us from debt, to claim vengeance on sin and its originator and to enable new life is clear.

God in His mercy sent Jesus to become a Man – to become one of us – so that He could be our Kinsman. As Holy God, He couldn't be our Kinsman, yet as the God-man He became our Kinsman and can relate to us as frail mankind (Hebrews 4:15). Hebrews 4:15 also shows how Jesus could fulfil one of the other criteria for a Kinsman-Redeemer – He was without sin. Only a perfect, sinless One could pay the sin-debt for the world. Had Jesus sinned, He could only have paid His own sin-debt. But as a sinless substitute, He could meet the price required for the whole world. And the Bible shows us that the Lord was willing (Luke 9:51; 22:42). Why was He willing to die on my behalf? Hebrews 12:2 tells us that it was "for the joy that was set before Him" that He "endured the cross, despising the shame". The Lord Jesus knew that His work on the cross would result in the salvation and redemption of many, and He counted that as such joy that He would willingly endure the pain, shame and humiliation of death on the cross – for me!

Boaz, acting as kinsman-redeemer for Ruth and for Naomi, is an image of the greater Kinsman-Redeemer. Boaz, acting as kinsman-redeemer, points us to Jesus.

Blessing to Jew and Gentile – blessing to the world

Genesis begins the story of how God called out one man, Abraham, and then his family and the nation that they became, to be His special people, for a particular relationship with Him and for blessing. Yet it was never God's intention that blessing should be restricted to just one family. Instead, He purposed that, through His special relationship with this one nation, all the world would be blessed. In His cov[nant to Abraham, God promised that "all peoples on earth shall be blessed" through Abraham (Genesis 12:3), reiterating this after the testing of Abraham: "In your seed all the nations of the earth shall be blessed, because you have obeyed My voice" (Genesis 22:18). The Old Testament shows us that, while relationship with God centred around the Israelites, Gentiles could receive blessing through their interaction with Israel and be adopted into the family of faith through their personal faith in God. We see this in the lives of Rahab and Ruth in particular.

In this dispensation - the way in which God is dealing with mankind in our times - we know that God accepts all on the basis of faith in His redemptive work on the cross. Now, salvation is offered to all people without discrimination – Jew or Gentile – and all are one in Christ (Galatians 3:28; Colossians 3:11). God's desire is for all to be saved, regardless of background (1 Timothy 2:4). In the Great Commission, Jesus instructed His disciple to "go ... and make disciples of all the nations" (Matthew 28:19). The Gospel isn't just for those of a certain social group or any other classification into which we put people. The Gospel is for all people, everywhere – for the whole world. Am I doing my part in reaching out to those around me so that they may be blessed? Does my relationship with God so affect my life that others see the difference He makes and are drawn to Him?

The Book of Ruth shows how one Gentile woman was blessed and drawn into a relationship with God because of her faith. The Book of Ruth reminds us of how God wants to bless those of every nation. The Book of Ruth reminds us that Jesus' work is for all.

Rest

The theme of searching for a resting place appears in chapter 1 of Ruth: "The LORD grant that you may find rest, each in the house of her husband" (v. 9). Again, in 3:1, Naomi brings up the issue of finding a resting place for Ruth – "shall I not seek security for you?". In these verses, closely related Hebrew words are used, and translated as "rest" or "security". The idea is of a resting place, a secure place of repose and safety. The root of these words is not the same as that used for Sabbath rest, the act of resting from work and toil (also a theme that runs throughout the Bible), but rather a reference to a place. It is first used in Genesis 8:9. After the flood waters had covered the earth and the rain had ceased, Noah sent a raven and then a dove out of the Ark to see if the ground had dried up. When the dove was first sent out, we're told that "the dove found no resting place for the sole of her foot, and she returned into the ark to him, for the waters were on the face of the whole earth" (v. 9). As the Old Testament progresses, we find that the resting place was part of the inheritance God promised to Israel (Deuteronomy 12:9). God wanted His people to have a resting place where He could dwell with them. The Israelites are warned that they will not find their resting place amongst the nations (Deuteronomy 28:65; Lamentations 1:3). On the contrary, God could provide their resting place and had promised to do so (1 Kings 8:56; Psalm 116:7; Isaiah 11:10; 28:12; 32:18) although disobedience would risk their being excluded from His resting place (Psalm 95:11). Similarly, the Tabernacle and Temple are referred to as the resting place for the Ark and for God (1 Chronicles 6:31; Psalm 132:8, 14).

When Naomi spoke of finding a resting place for Ruth, she meant finding a husband and home for her. Initially, Naomi suggested finding rest with a Moabite husband, but we know this can never be for one following the God of Israel, so Ruth refuses to go back to Moab and instead remains with her mother-in-law. Naomi's second attempt is better – seeking rest with the kinsman-redeemer. As an image of the true Kinsman-Redeemer, Boaz was the one place Ruth should look for and find her resting place. God still promises a resting place for those who trust in Him. Jesus' call remains true: "Come to Me ... and I will give you rest" (Matthew 11:28). Jesus has promised that He is preparing a place for us and that He will come again to take us to dwell with Him there (John 14:2, 3). Do I try to make my resting place and look for security in the things of this world or do I seek it in the Lord? Do I, like Ruth, find my refuge under His wings?

The Book of Ruth reminds us that our resting place is found in our Kinsman-Redeemer. The Book of Ruth reminds us that Jesus is the place where I find rest and security.

Hope to come

As we've studied the Book of Ruth, we've come across glimmerings of future hope, foreshadowings of what's yet to come. In chapter 1, it was how Naomi and Ruth arrived back in Bethlehem "at the beginning of barley harvest" (1:22), pointing us to the hope of a change in circumstances as the famine is now ended and the hope that other circumstances would soon change for our widows. In chapter 2, we're teased with the details about Boaz in verse 1, seemingly breaking early into the flow of the story, but hinting that there may indeed be hope for another change in circumstances for Naomi, and Ruth in particular. Further, we get the comment that Ruth "happened to come to the part of the field belonging to Boaz" (v. 3), consolidating our belief that God is at work behind the scenes, for blessing. Throughout chapters 2 and 3, we see Boaz going above and beyond his requirements to provide for Ruth and Naomi's needs, affording the hope that he will do more than supply food but will meet their deeper needs. Finally, in chapter 4, we see the genealogies closing the book with the hope of the great King of Israel, David, and subsequent hope of the coming Messiah.

Like the Book of Ruth, the whole Bible is full of hints and promises of what's to come and what God's great plan of salvation involves. Right after the Fall, God gives His first 'teaser' of His plan by telling of the One to come who would "crush [Satan's] head" (Genesis 3:15, NIV) and defeat him forever. We see examples of God providing salvation through Moses, Joshua, the judges, and others. The books of the prophets are full of promises for the coming of the Messiah, who He was and what

His mission would be. Even Caiaphas unknowingly predicted how Jesus' death would be for the benefit of the nation (and beyond) (John 11:49-50). And yet the promises of the Bible don't stop at that point. There are promises yet to be fulfilled that relate to our future. God has a future planned for us that we can be sure will come to pass. One day, Christ will return and call all of His followers home to Himself. Those who trust in Him will enjoy everlasting life with Him in heaven. Those who reject Him in this life will be punished. God has told us what will happen and we need to act on that information. For those who are His, this should bring us great joy as we await His return, aware of all the blessings that are ours. Don't be one of those who will miss out on these blessings by rejecting Him in this life!

The Book of Ruth reminds us of the hope we have for the future. The Book of Ruth points us to the hope we have in Jesus.

Creation-Fall-Redemption-Restoration

As discussed in the Introduction, the Book of Ruth follows a structure common to the Bible narratives as well as one being used in storytelling today. The structure of creation-fall-redemption-restoration is often used to describe the structure of the whole of the Bible and of God's dealings with mankind.

Creation: God creates the world and everything in it. Mankind was created, and enjoyed a relationship with their Creator-God. He saw that His creation was very good. (Introduction)

Fall: Man sinned by disobeying God. This broke the relationship between God and mankind (spiritual death) and brought physical death into God's created world. Adam and Eve's sin had consequences on all of creation. (Crisis)

Redemption: God had a plan for redeeming mankind and restoring the relationship that had been broken. Sin was punishable by death, but God planned a way by which One could die in the place of mankind. Much of the Old Testament points to this in prophecies and images. God became a Man, Jesus Christ, who died so that salvation could be offered to mankind. (The way of making things right)

Restoration: By faith in Christ's redemptive work, men and women can be saved from the penalty their sin deserved. Their relationship with God is restored. Not only this, God also provides abundant blessings for those who believe, both now and in eternity. ("Happily, ever after", restoring what was lost/ blessings)

The structure of Ruth reminds us of God's big plan of redemption and restoration. The structure of the Book of Ruth points us to Jesus.

Points for further thought and action

- ❖ Boaz as kinsman-redeemer is a picture of Jesus. Is Jesus your Kinsman-Redeemer? If not, will you accept Him as such today?

- ❖ God wants to bless all nations – the work of Jesus is for all. What part are you playing in spreading the Gospel to all?

- ❖ The only true resting-place is in Jesus. Are you searching for rest elsewhere? Is Jesus your resting-place?

- ❖ We have hope for the future because of Jesus. How does this hope affect your life? Are you living in the light of this hope?

- ❖ God's big plan is for redemption and restoration. How have you seen this in your life? How can you be part of His plan of the redemption and restoration of others?

Bibliography and tools used

Printed resources

Baxter, J.S. *Explore the Book.* Grand Rapids, Michigan: Zondervan, 1960

Flanigan, J.M. *What the Bible Teaches: Ruth.* Kilmarnock: John Ritchie, 2009

Grant, F.W. *The Numerical Bible.* Neptune, New Jersey: Loizeaux Brothers, 1932

Guthrie, D. J., A. Motyer, A.M. Stibbs and D.J. Wiseman *The New Bible Commentary 3rd ed. revised.* Leicester: IVP, 1980

Harlow, R.E. *Winning & Losing. Studies in Joshua, Judges, and Ruth.* Port Colborne, Ontario: Everyday Publications Inc., 2005

Henry, M. *A Commentary on the Whole Bible, Volume 2 Joshua to Esther.* Iowa Falls, Iowa: World Bible Publishers, 1968-88

Higgs, L.C. *The Girl's Still Got It.* Colorado Springs, Colorado: WaterBrook Press, 2012

MacDonald, W. *Believer's Bible Commentary.* Nashville, Tennessee: Nelson, 1989

McGee, J.V. *Ruth and Esther: Women of Faith.* Nashville, Tennessee: Nelson, 1988

Mawson, J.T. *How to Overcome – being talks on Judges.* Crewe: STP, 2009

Moorhouse, H. *Collective writings and Sermons of Henry Moorhouse.* Port Colborne, Ontario: Gospel Folio Press, 2010

Nielson, K.B. *Ruth and Esther: a 12-week study.* Wheaton, Illinois: Crossway, 2014

Packer, J.I. and D. Williams *The Bible Application Handbook.* Guildford, Surrey: Eagle, 1999

Ridout, S. *Judges and Ruth.* Neptune, New Jersey: Loizeaux Brothers, 1981

Rossier, H.L. *Meditations on Ruth & 1 Samuel.* Beamsville, Ontario: Believers Bookshelf Canada, 1994

Sheldon, B.W. *The Messiah and the Feasts of Israel.* Port Colborne, Ontario: Gospel Folio Press, 2007

Smith, H. *The Book of Ruth.* Belfast: Words of Truth, n.d.

Strong, J., J.R. Kohlenberger III and J.A. Swanson (ed.) *The Strongest Strong's Exhaustive Concordance of the Bible.* Grand Rapids, Michigan: Zondervan, 2001

Ulrich, D.R. *From Famine to Fullness.* Phillipsburg, New Jersey: P&R Publishing, 2007

Vander Velde, F. *Women of the Bible.* Grand Rapids, Michigan: Kregel Publications, 2000

Walton, J.H., M.L. Strauss and T. Cooper Jr. *The Essential Bible Companion.* Grand Rapids, Michigan: Zondervan, 2006

Walvoord, J.F. and R.B. Zuck *The Bible Knowledge Commentary.* Colorado Springs, Colorado: David C. Cook, 1985

Wiersbe, W.W. *The Wiersbe Bible Commentary.* Colorado Springs, Colorado: David C. Cook, 2007

Zuck, R.B. *Basic Bible Interpretation.* Colorado Springs, Colorado: David C Cook, 1991

E-resources

https://www.biblegateway.com

https://www.scripture4all.org/OnlineInterlinear/Hebrew_Index.htm

https://thebibleproject.com/explore/ruth/

About the author

Katherine was born in Liverpool and was taught and shown the importance of personally studying and understanding the Bible by her parents and grandparents. She has practiced as a midwife in the north, and more latterly the south, of England. She is married to Samuel and is the mother of two young children. Her hope is that this book will help encourage personal study of the scriptures and biblical literacy among its readers.

www.ingramcontent.com/pod-product-compliance
Lightning Source LLC
Chambersburg PA
CBHW061342040426
42444CB00011B/3050